BLACK BOY,
CREATE!

AN INTERACTIVE GUIDE TO BUILDING
VISION, BRAND, AND SOCIAL INFLUENCE

DAVID GEORGE

David George & Co., LLC

Los Angeles

Black Boy, Create!

David George & Co., LLC
Los Angeles

Copyright © 2022 by David George

For permissions contact:
david@davidgeorgeco.com

ISBN: 979-8-9862448-0-8 (Hardcover)
ISBN: 979-8-9862448-1-5 (Paperback)
ISBN: 979-8-9862448-2-2 (eBook)

CONTENTS

INTRODUCTION

Black cool has made and popularized some of today's biggest trends. From art and language to fashion and Hip Hop, the Renegade, the Whoa, and every major TikTok dance you can think of; black creators are driving digital and modern popular culture. Further, social platforms are where many of today's young, ambitious creators are making their names and fortunes—while part of this demographic is standing on the sidelines debating whether they will just be consumers or become producers. Accordingly, the content in this book is embedded in the ethos of the creator economy—laying a foundation for the next generation to discover what's at the intersection of talent, creativity, and technology.

This book is for creative black boys who are on the come up and can benefit from hearing a different story. Boys who understand that before there was a Ye, there was Kanye Omari West from Chicago—one of the many visionaries who broke the monolithic stereotype around the ability of black men in arts and entrepreneurship.

This book will empower black boys to see opportunity in a digital-first world and take the steps to determine their own future. #SupportCreativeBlackBoys

FANTASY, CREATIVITY, AND
FEARLESS JOY WILL BECOME
A NECESSARY ANTIDOTE
FOR THIS GENERATION'S
VERY SURVIVAL.

63%

OF 14-TO-27-YEAR-OLDS BELIEVE THAT BREAKING THE MOLD IS MORE IMPORTANT THAN STABILITY.

CHAPTER **ONE**

THE DIGITAL ERA

Today's generation—from school-aged children to the fearless Gen Z—is heavily influenced by popular culture and know that they want to be some type of Influencer or Creator one day. For the past decade, they've witnessed a digital revolution, and vast amounts of people who look just like them use online platforms to communicate with the world and eventually get paid to be themselves.

Although **personal branding** and content creation still may not be a part of the traditional school curriculum, kids today know that making videos on TikTok and You-Tube, posting on Instagram, or streaming on Twitch are legitimate career paths. Therefore, the future generation of creators are ditching anything that doesn't align with their desires of building a following and creating a popular online presence—the new American dream.

PERSONAL **BRAND:**

A widely-recognized and largely-uniform perception or impression of an individual based on their experience, expertise, competencies, actions, and/or achievements within a community, industry, or the marketplace at large.

Unfortunately, unless they come from entrepreneurial families, or are surrounded by people who truly 'get' this industry, most parents or guardians will respond with negativity or some form of cynicism around the topic. But let us not forget that there was a generation of people who also didn't respond well to the birth of the internet in the '80s. They resisted learning email and REALLY didn't trust the idea of entering their credit card information online. Four decades later, the internet has become our strongest form of human communication and where over 80 percent of consumers shop and do business. So, parents, this is your warning to not be one of those people who always say "no" to things you don't understand. Anyone born in the mid '90s to today are native users of new social networks and grew up in a technological wonderland.

I say this because, most creators can recall a time where someone in their life tried to convince them that their passion would never be "a real job". It happened to me. Sadly, one of the top reasons people give up on their dreams, is because they fear being judged by their loved ones. Judged for failing.

Whether you have been a victim of this, or identify as a dream killer yourself, I am not saying that you or the people around you are bad. However, there may be a lack of understanding about what kind of world we live in today. It's the kind where a 12-year-old kid and their mom can build a lucrative business, by creating a TikTok channel. A channel that lands them endorsement deals, entertainment contracts, and more. There's no doubt that the world will continue to evolve in this direction. If you're paying attention to what is actually happening in the world, this should come as no surprise.

The influencer success story has become a lot less unusual and more mainstream.

I became immersed in the influencer marketing world when I moved to Los Angeles in 2016. I became a Personal Assistant to a popular creator—who at the time had about 8 million followers across Instagram and YouTube. Digital attention helped them generate income in the high six-figures, annually. If you're anything like me, you're curious to learn how they achieved this. Well, I'll tell you. They **monetized** original content on the social platforms and collaborated with consumer goods brands through partnerships known as **brand deals**.

MONETIZE:

earn revenue from (an asset, business, etc.).

BRAND DEAL:

a paid partnership between creators and brands and is sometimes referred to as a "brand sponsorship," too.

Witnessing this first-hand showed me that using social media to amplify or build a business around your passion was not only realistic, but very possible. So, for years, I have been locked in on this space and have committed to learning from some of the most followed people in the creator community. Additionally, I have worked with some of the largest entertainment, lifestyle, and consumer brands. Leveraging relationships with media, celebrities, brand partners, community influencers, and tastemakers to create cross-cultural digital and **influencer marketing campaigns**.

INFLUENCER MARKETING CAMPAIGNS:

A type of social media marketing strategy that sees brands collaborate with trusted influencers or content creators with the power to affect how their audience makes purchasing decisions.

I got my start in marketing as an intern at mass media company ViacomCBS. Like most students from underserved communities, I could not afford to do a ton of unpaid internships. I needed most of my free time to work and make money, so senior year of college I decided to stack all my courses on two days of the week. This created space to get the experience I needed to launch a respected career in marketing. Today, I create marketing strategies for a company that is a global leader in kid's toys and entertainment—developing digital-first partnerships with influencers and celebrity talent.

As a kid, I was very book smart, but I had a natural talent for the visual and performing arts that I knew would carve a career path for me one day. I really shined when I was able to express myself through some form of a creative medium; so much that I would find ways to get involved with youth arts organizations in my community. Around 11 or 12 years old I became extremely determined to be cast on Nickelodeon. I was obsessed with the sketch comedy show 'All That', where I witnessed young and talented kids who looked like me live out their wildest dreams.

But I knew things like that didn't just happen.

That's when I came up with the bright idea to go through the yellow pages and send handwritten letters to any and every listing that had "talent" "studio" or "production" in its title. I would send them a biography (that outlined who I was and what my dreams were), a photo, and sometimes even a story or song that I wrote. I believed in myself that much.

Somehow, one of the letters that I addressed to "a studio near Boston" got delivered to Madeleine Steczynski (Founder of non-profit cultural organization ZUMiX). She called me with a special invitation to join my first ever arts and music program. By 14, I discovered the OrigiNation Cultural Arts Center (a nonprofit performing arts organization in Roxbury, Massachusetts). This is where I found community through my passion for dance and felt empowered to be a leader. I am so thankful for Shaumba-Yandje, Musau, Muadi, and the entire Dibinga family for recognizing my potential and for pushing me every step of the way.

While I am grateful that I was able to lead myself at such a young age, I am aware that not every kid is. Some kids will never discover their fullest potential without guidance and support. I say this to put a signal on your radar, that there are millions of kids out there who learn what they are good at very early in life. They need your help to go all the way. Kid or adult, you can use a personal brand, i.e. who you are, to thrive within an industry, promote a business, or be the business. The Kardashians have been doing it for years; now it's your turn.

I titled this book "Black Boy, Create!" because I find that black boys are often the least expected to succeed in this country outside of sports and entertainment. Statistics show that the U.S. education system continues to fail black male students in underserved communities. As a result, the dropout rate for black students remains higher than that for white students, according to the National School Boards Association. This is not because we don't possess the ability to learn, but because many black students, like myself, grow up in poverty. What we are being taught about success in schools doesn't reflect the people or community around us. Creative black boys are not being reached and are yearning to be exposed to success stories that go beyond the basketball court and football field. This book is going to introduce the power of vision and personal branding through different characters. Characters whose stories are inspired by some of the most innovative black men and boys of this generation. I believe this creates an opportunity for those who need it, to see themselves through different role models. To visualize how to blaze a similar path. This book is also meant to serve as a guide to help parents or guardians recognize that their kid may be a creative thinker or unique problem-solver. A guide on how they can inspire them to use their creativity and imagination to go as far as they want to go.

I think it's important to point out that the success stories referenced in this book had nothing to do with luck or all the things we believe give some people more of a competitive advantage over others. Examples, such as cultural background, upbringing, nepotism, or college education. Rather it had everything to do with their appreciation for technology today and willingness to do the work. If you take away any value, I hope that you will use this book as a tool to help yourself or another individual in your life discover who and what they can be.

The realist in me needs to remind you that what worked for them won't necessarily work for you. This journey will require a high level of self-awareness and thoughtful application. The content in this book will offer a set of universal principles and dissect major platforms. Providing the most up-to-date information on how to best leverage the internet to make content and amplify your creativity. Additionally, I will offer theoretical and tactical advice on how to grow as a creator, develop a community, and earn a living doing what you love.

But first, let's get clear about a few things:

- In the words of Gary Vee, a book like this is for two audiences: One, for people who know they are born to use their voice and create content that impacts the world. Two, for those who just want to become extremely tech-savvy. During this process, you might discover you are better behind the camera and can help other people and businesses maximize their digital engagement.

- Even if you follow everything, most people will not

become paid social media stars—Keep reading—
None of the people I will talk about later knew they
would either. They knew they were talented, willing
to try, and would be always true to themselves. Most
of them started with a 'why'. A sense of urgency and
ambitions to do enough to change their lives. You
don't need a ton of money to do this! With the explo-
sion of digital platforms, you already have the tools,
for free. If you own a smartphone, you can build a
digital brand, and this book can teach you how.

- I cannot make you more creative, but I hope to put
  you in the right frame of mind so that when you're
  ready to unleash your creativity, you know where to
  start.
- If you're happy with the path that you are currently
  on, great. This book was written for the people who
  are not, or just need a little more information to really take off. We no longer need to settle and do something tolerable to make money or follow our passion
  with the expectation we will be poor.

It's time to tell yourself a different story.

CHAPTER **TWO**

EXCELLENCE IS A MINDSET

I don't believe we can have a conversation about seeing possibility without having a conversation about mindset. I believe that getting what you want out of life begins with simply knowing that you can—do more, learn more, and most importantly, be more.

Let me explain.

I uploaded my first YouTube video in 2009. The platform was very popular in the dance community around this time, connecting dancers from all over the world. If you know anything about the entertainment industry, you know that the only talented people who got a shot at being discovered, or earned opportunities to work with celebrities, were those who could afford to move to big cities. Cities like Los Angeles or New York. Every dancer's dream is to star in music videos or go on tour with a major artist. Luckily for us, YouTube was making it possible for amateur dancers to be seen and build a reputation before making "the move". Otherwise, most risk becoming a small fish in a big pond.

I didn't know what it was called then, but this is where the concept of personal branding first stood out to me. Excited to "build our brands", my peers and I (shoutout to **@AyoKeenan**) would teach classes in our neighborhood and upload dance and choreography videos every week. Posting consistently proved to be the best way to keep my subscribers engaged. My highest performing video to date was to Rihanna and Drake's 2010 hit song "What's My Name", generating over 200K views. This was a big deal during early YouTube. My other content averaged 50K-100K+ views, capturing the attention of DanceOn, (the first online dance network) who invited me to become a paid partner on YouTube. As an 18-year-old kid who created these types of organic results, I thought I was "making it". I was ready to take the next step in my career.

Now it was time for the move.

It was a chilly summer night when I was scheduled to board a bus from Boston to New York City at midnight. It was just me, a pillow, and a suitcase.

I remember being excited to start a new chapter in the Big Apple, but I also remember feeling incredibly lonely. Earlier that evening, I threw myself a going away party. I invited some of my friends and family over to celebrate, before I went off to start my first semester at St. John's University. I don't quite remember everything that happened that night, but I remember my mom being the last person I hugged before getting in the car to go to the bus station. Just a hug though, no "I'll miss you" or words of encouragement. I guess I didn't realize how much that moment stuck with me until now. I've had thick skin all my life...it was how I avoided getting hurt. But, in that moment, I didn't feel seen or like the person who brought me into this world had any real expectations for me. Now that hurt.

Looking back, I think that maybe it was because I never openly discussed my plans for my life. By this time, I was doing exceptionally well academically, already completed two years of college, and was recognized as a young leader in my community. I thought it was obvious that I had all the makings of someone who could do anything he put his mind to. Plus, I had talent that earned me three appearances as a dancer on national television and over 3,000 subscribers on my YouTube channel. The perfect recipe for success in New York City, right?

Right. But if I didn't believe that to be true, I would have never gotten on the bus that night. I believed that I could "do more, learn more, and most importantly, be more". I believed that something different could happen.

The point is, I find that when we start to feel stuck, it's usually because we are telling ourselves the wrong story. We get caught up blaming our circumstances and sometimes expect others (like our parents) to believe in us more than we believe in ourselves. But the truth is, as individuals our minds are either programmed to succeed or to fail. Depending on how you're programmed, what you believe you can accomplish is what will inspire the actions you take. It doesn't work the other way around.

Champion thinkers know that good habits create opportunity and that bad habits don't.

So, here's my challenge for you. Understand that everything you do is an action towards something and know that you always have a choice. When things don't go your way, you can; 1, do nothing, let it get the best of you, and fall victim to your circumstances or 2, face the adversity head-on, move toward it, and make it a part of your story. I recommend option 2. Always choose to DO something.

NAVIGATION **POINT:**

Before you start to evaluate where you fall on the victory scale, first, understand that the way you think may not entirely be your fault. In most cases, the thoughts, and beliefs we inherit are a direct reflection of the people who influenced us growing up. This includes our parents, teachers, people on tv, and even our friends. External factors have the biggest influence on our world view, which plays a role in shaping who we become. The upside is whether you've received positive or negative programming, we all can change.

This would be a great time to take out a journal or piece of paper and complete the following exercise:

- Identify a champion in your life. This could be someone you know personally or a public figure that inspires you.
- Decide to understand the way champions think. What habits does this person demonstrate that you believe makes them successful? What can you ob-

serve is special about the way that they think?

- Write down your learnings and practice applying them to cultivate your own champion mindset.

CHAPTER **THREE**

BECOME AWARE OF SELF

Imagine growing up, a young Black male in one of the 'worst three' ranked neighborhoods in Boston, Massachusetts. In an environment that encourages you to "just get a job" because you are "too poor" to go to college. Frustrated with the dismal examples being set by your surroundings and in some cases, your family. Disappointed in the lack of resources available to help you access a better life. Being more interested in music lyrics than what "normal" boys were "supposed" to do. Just making it to 18 was a hefty feat. But, to have the moral fortitude to delve completely into my art, despite what the norm may have been, and allow it to usher me to a life walking in my purpose... Now that, was a dream.

I fully admit that MTV and popular culture played a huge role in shaping who I am today.

Rhythm has coursed through my veins since the music video channel heyday, manifesting the moment I hit the stage at a local talent show for the first time at 8-years old.

As we established in the last chapter, before I discovered I was a marketer, I spent most of my life focused on becoming a professional dancer. At 16, I created my first dance video, learned to build websites, and made a highlight **reel** that compiled all my creative work from over the years.

REEL:

A short video showcasing a person's previous work and/or current capabilities.

It was crappy, but I was proud of it, and I knew that I would get better with time. I was never afraid to try new things and believe me, I tried my hand at a lot of things to figure out who I am. My philosophy was simple, "if you never try, you'll never know". But of course, there were challenges along the way.

I transferred colleges twice before landing at St. John's University. This is where I studied Business Management and Marketing, while pursuing a professional dance career on the side. Amongst the New York entertainment scene, I was regarded not only as a Dancer, but a go-getter who possessed the wherewithal to make things happen. Driven by an underlying desire to start my own business, I turned my skills into a multi-faceted hustle. I was the go-to guy for everything from choreography, to editing reels, advising on creative shoots, music edits, and more. My goal was to create as many avenues as possible to make money and gain experience while I figured out the dance thing.

Somewhere in the mix, I did get caught up helping other people so often that I wasn't doing the one thing I set out to do—become a dancer. I developed some great skills, but what I declared as my "dream" started to fade to the back, and it showed in the results. I was lost in the dance industry and just didn't understand how it worked. Also, due to finances, I was barely training or in classes. Therefore, I wasn't involved in the community, I didn't have an agent, my attitude sucked, and I was only making enough money to pay rent.

One day, while I was ranting about my experience during a work-study shift at Broadway Dance Center, my co-worker asked me if I thought I was putting in one hundred percent to achieve my goals. That was the moment I realized that the problem could be me and not the industry. I wanted this huge outcome, but I was only giving about thirty percent of my energy to my goals, not one hundred. Part of it was resistance to the work that needed to be done and the other part was spent... surviving.

I had to support myself, so I had a part-time job in retail and taught dance classes to kids during the day. I used any extra time I had to attend free seminars and revisit the information I learned in business school. I got better at marketing, networking, and showcasing my skills in a way that helped me build a personal brand. In fact, I understood that by building a **brand,** I was building a business by default. A name, image, and likeness that I could leverage down the line.

BRAND:

A business and marketing concept that helps people identify a particular company, product, or individual.

The good news is my new strategy worked. After about six months of consistent execution, I signed with bloc NYC, a top talent agency for dancers and choreographers. Within my first two years of being a signed dancer, I booked a few gigs across TV, stage, music video, commercial, and print. I was very good at finding ways to package myself (aka market my personal brand) and create new opportunities. But even then, I still felt resistance.

Like most young adults, I set a lot of, "Before I'm 30…" goals, which I believe heightened my sense of urgency to take risks and get things done. It's like when you give yourself two hours to complete a task compared to two days. You'll meet your deadline in either scenario, but one pushes you to do it right now, while the other feeds your procrastination. I personally don't think there is anything wrong with giving yourself deadlines if you use them as a motivator and not as a reason to put unnecessary pressure on yourself. For me, 30 was only five years away and it felt like a good time to check-in with myself.

With all that I was able to accomplish up until that point, there were still days that I would question whether I saw dance in my future. At any moment a cancelled gig or an injury could set you back, and that's not an enjoyable feeling for someone living in one of the most expensive cities in the world. That was the reason for my lack of enthusiasm at times. Again, tapping into different skills is how I learned that being creative is not one-dimensional. At the same time, I knew I had to eventually pick my niche and stick to it. I loved to perform, but I also grew an affinity for the creative process and business side of the industry. Checking in leads to greater self-awareness. I realized that what I really wanted to do, was to collaborate with people on their visions and create amazing content. That required me to change the path, but not the goal of getting paid to be creative. It's also what led me to becoming an **intrapreneur** at one of the biggest fashion brands in the world. More on this in the next chapter.

INTRA**PRENEUR:**

An employee who is tasked with developing an innovative idea or project within a company.

Take a moment and think about your desired outcome.

- What does one hundred percent of effort look like towards achieving that goal?
- Do you notice any distractions that may be navigating you away from where you want to be? Write it down and be very specific about the steps you need to take.
- If you don't know where to start, think about the person you selected in Chapter 2. Do they have interviews you can watch and learn about their process? Did they write a book about their journey or challenges?

Studying people who have done it before is the best way to determine your next step.

CHAPTER **FOUR**

SEE THE OPPORTUNITY TO SEIZE THE OPPORTUNITY

After I graduated college, I was broke...I mean BROKE. So I decided to get a part-time job as a sales associate, beginning my journey in fashion in 2013.

While browsing an internal job board at work one day, I noticed an untitled opening for "someone passionate about social media". That's literally what it said, no formal title and no job description. It's worth noting that this was also a time when social networks like Instagram were only a few years old and big corporations were still figuring out how they wanted to exist on the platforms. Knowing that I immediately saw a small **window of opportunity** and approached my then manager to learn more about the position. I don't know whether he took me seriously or not, but I had to ask about this opportunity for almost a month before anything happened. My curiosity eventually led to a conversation with the store director (who told me that I was the only person that inquired about the job post by the way) he believed in me, and we decided that we would build this role together. We later developed the Social Stylist, a beta digital marketing role designed to empower the style, creativity, and voice of passionate employees.

WINDOW OF **OPPORTUNITY:**

A chance to do something that will only last for a short time – it needs to be taken advantage of rapidly; before the window is gone. It is a very short time frame during which an opportunity must be seized or lost.

The opportunity I recognized was a chance to blend my passions for style and performance. A career driving opportunity for myself and a marketing approach I knew could support the brand's goal of reaching young consumers. My manager explained to me that the company was trying to find a savvy way to approach social media and reach millennials online. I thought, "I'm a millennial". So, I assessed the situation like, okay, if I didn't work here, what would make this brand's products more appealing to me? What type of story do I need to hear, and what kind of visual presentation would I like to see?

The fashion community was obsessed with blogging and look-books during this time, so I decided that would be the inspiration for our first project around the new collection. Believe me when I tell you that there is so much value in leaning into the visibility of existing trends. You must know the interests of the people you are trying to reach and how they are connecting around those interests. My strategy was to take a brand known for basics and show that they could adapt to the millennial's fashion preference, embracing the movement towards individuality. The company was already doing a great job at meeting the market's demand for logo-less but high-quality fashion items. We just needed to encourage our audience to explore their personal style and allow us to be a part of their fashion experiences.

I **crowd-sourced** the entire project by putting ads on Instagram, Facebook, Craigslist, Model Mayhem, and even asked for favors within my personal network–– leveraging the brand's name to put together a professional-level team. We collaborated with all local talent, including photographers, models, stylists, hair and make-up artists, and passionate brand enthusiasts, to create something everyone felt like they were a part of. By doing this, we were making great content and cultivating a community that, by default, helped build our social media presence and drive follower growth.

CROWD-SOURCE:

Obtain (information or input into a particular task or project) by enlisting the services of a large number of people, either paid or unpaid, typically via the internet.

For the consumers who preferred video, we introduced a YouTube series not too long after that. Launching a campaign that told stories around how fashion can enrich the lives of everyday people. It was viewed over 135K times, capturing the spirit of the brand's past with a refreshingly forward spin. Again, without an actual budget, I relied on my own creative skills to pull off what, by all accounts looked like legit commercials. The final product wasn't perfect, but I did it, and it showed my team that I had a vision. That was why they chose to invest in me.

I went on to partner with the company for their 'Brand Vision Experience', which was a conference intended to inspire the top leaders at the company. I cast and co-choreographed an energetic piece, nostalgic of the brand's commercials we all loved in the 90s (quick shout-out to Aurelia Michael, who was my right hand throughout the entire process). This was also my first touring experience, presenting work in Las Vegas, San Francisco, and of course, New York City. Making this the last project I completed at that company before exiting in the fall of 2016.

NAVIGATION **POINT:**

I consider foresight to be my hidden superpower. The ability to think ahead prepares me to take advantage of all the new opportunities that rapid social and technological progress creates. In this exercise I would like for you to brainstorm where there may be windows of opportunity in your life. Are you currently working for a company or in a space where there are opportunities to be an intrapreneur?

- Take a second to outline the potential opportunity. What is something that you do extremely well that could be brought to the table?
- Who do you need to talk to about it and when are you going to reach out to them?

Consider maximizing the opportunities that are in front of you, to drive innovation before stepping out on your own. It will boost your skills and overall confidence as you work towards building your profile as a creator.

Bringing YOU to the table is extremely valuable in today's market. It will also help you create the ultimate leverage for your next opportunity.

CHAPTER **FIVE**

CONTENT IS *KING*

Being a YouTuber, Snapchat or Instagram influencer was officially at its peak in 2016, and all the social stars were moving to Los Angeles. I wanted to be a part of how marketing was evolving, so that's where I went next.

Marketing was becoming more human, and millions of people were creating digital profiles to show off their talent, personality, or tell captivating stories through images and videos. Creating content, aka, the art of **storytelling** is not difficult or complex. It just requires lots of practice and less overthinking.

STORYTELLING:

An interactive art of using words and actions to reveal the elements and images of a story while encouraging the listener's imagination.

A story is essentially the key driver that keeps us interested in the people and brands we love today. Whether it's the messaging in their content, or the visuals and characters we see when we interact with them, each brand is intentional from the start. It's how they capture our attention, and those strategic decisions are made for a reason. They want you to connect with them because it leads to awareness. Awareness drives attention and that can be monetized.

The takeaway is your content should also tell a story. When people engage with you online, what do they see? Is it just your fit of the day, or are you creating something that makes people want to spend the day WITH you? Is your fashion apparel special just because you created it? Or does it stand for something we ALL can be a part of?

NAVIGATION **POINT:**

Take out your journal and start brainstorming around the voice, style, and objective you want your content to have:

- Are you trying to build a personal brand, a business brand, a lifestyle, or entertainment brand?
- Do you consider yourself an expert of a specific topic or subject matter that you can talk about?
- Do you live a lifestyle that's worth documenting and would be appealing to a specific community?
- Do you have a fascinating creative ability (i.e. video editing or photography skills) or do you prefer to capture raw unfiltered content?
- Do you love to participate in cultural trends or support social causes?

Answering these questions will help you craft your vision for your brand. Every great story begins with a vision.

It's best to try and resonate with a community and deliver anticipated, personal, and relevant messages that people want to get. Too many people get lost running a hype show today. Trying to sell perception over authentically building something that will last. It's important to establish roots and anchor your work deeply in the lifestyle, dreams, and desires of those you seek to serve. It's about influencing people for the better, creating content you can be proud of, and being a driver of the market. Not simply being market-driven.

I've learned from different leaders in the marketing space, that if you want to have influence, begin by making culture i.e. "People like us do things like this". Culture beats strategy so much that culture *is* strategy. However, your first job is to define "us". The more specific and the more connected the "us", the better. There is no universal culture that defines us all.

But how do you shape or make a culture?

Start by mapping out and understanding the worldview of the culture you seek to change. Then, focus all of your energy on building and living a story that will resonate with this group—the culture we are seeking to change. The creators who drive impact are the ones who take initiative in not only reaching, but in changing the expectations of the people who follow them. They introduce them to a better or unexpected way of doing something, and they have influence over what they choose to tell and show each other. At the heart of every culture is an exclusive cohort that establishes an emotional connection with its members.

"People like us do _____.
Join this community and you gain _____.
Walk away and you lose it."

LET'S RECAP:

- **Stories demand an emotional investment:** Create things worth making, with a story worth telling and a purpose worth talking about.
- **Stories bring energy to the message:** Design and curate it in a way that a niche group of people will particularly benefit from and care about.
- **Stories pique and hold interest:** Tell a story that matches the built-in narrative and interests of that tiny group of people and clearly identifies the smallest viable market.
- **Stories cause us to take action:** Use social media to spread the word and show up in the space—regularly, consistently, and honestly.

Regardless of the type of brand you desire to build, the truth is, you must get out there and make stuff. Ultimately, the audience decides what's "good", and you will not be able to build an effective content strategy until you have real data that tells you what's working FOR YOU. Yes, your content should offer value to a specific audience, and you must be intentional with how you use it to communicate to the world. But only AFTER you've tested different types of posts. Production quality is not super important in the beginning; getting things out there to test is.

From the videos and images that you create, to your captions and the overall look of your social media profiles, all of it should work together as a team to tell a part of your story. Commit to it, and it will begin to unfold organically into an online brand that is recognizable. A brand that most importantly speaks to the identity of your audience.

CHAPTER **SIX**

WHO GETS TO BE AN INFLUENCER?

Influencer marketing is a promotional strategy in which focus is placed on specific key individuals or types of individuals, rather than the target market as a whole. It involves a brand collaborating with a public figure or online personality to market one of its products or services. The influencer economy is no longer something the world can ignore and has become a billion-dollar industry, growing beyond $15 billion. Even global brands understand its value, with about 75% of them dedicating a large budget to influencer marketing in the new digital era. When I mention "Influencers" from this point forward, I am also talking about content creators, career professionals, and entrepreneurs who have a strong digital presence.

Influencers, unlike celebrities, can be anyone and from anywhere. In every industry, there are influential people. Some will have thousands (if not millions) of followers, but in the coming years, many will seem more like ordinary people with less than 10,000 followers in some cases. Yet, they will have developed a reputation for building community or being the experts in their field. They are the go-to people for niche groups, and the people who make the most engaging social posts around the things they're most passionate about. They share the best pictures, make the most entertaining videos, and drive the most impactful social conversations. Most of all, they drive engagement. Engagement equals attention, and companies will always be willing to team up with people who know how to capture and retain attention.

Contrary to popular belief, influencer marketing does not only focus on mega endorsements. Micro-influencers are just as effective for delivering successful results depending on the goals of the campaign. Again, these are ordinary people who have built up a solid social media following.

INFLUENCER HIERARCHY:

Mega-Influencers	*Social superstars with 1 million-plus followers.*
Macro-Influencers	*Influencers between 100,000 and 1 million followers.*
Micro-Influencers	*Someone who has between 1,000 and 100,000 followers. While their following may be small(ish), their authenticity and engagement are high.*
Nano-Influencers	*Somebody with fewer than 1,000 followers who have immense influence with a comparatively narrow niche.*

As an influencer, your goal should be to build an online audience of people you can authentically engage and persuade to make decisions through your personal interests. Your job is to figure out which type of content resonates best with the audience you wish to serve, and if you choose to monetize that, which brands align with the message you are trying to communicate. Influencers increase their earning potential once a brand can identify what value they bring to the market and establish a need for that value. This could be bringing in a new audience for the brand, helping them launch a targeted campaign, or a strategic partnership as a **brand ambassador** for a specific product or service.

BRAND AMBASSADOR:

A person hired by a company to bring its products, messaging, and brand image to the community.

For decades, many industries have made billions of dollars by leveraging the name, image, and likeness (NIL) of individuals like fashion models and college athletes who were not empowered to monetize their own talents. However, we are seeing more and more people embrace the new world of the NIL era and sign deals with their favorite brands. This means they will earn profits to produce unique content and experiences that align with earned and paid media strategies, PR initiatives, and editorial moments. All of which help brands amplify their messages and drive sales.

Let's dive deeper into this subject by taking a closer look at the different types of influencer marketing tactics.

PRODUCT OR
SERVICE ENDORSEMENTS:

One of the top ways an influencer can get paid, is through product or service endorsements. For beginners, an endorsement is a public declaration from a person or organization in support of a brand's message, products or services. Consumer brands that offer products that empower the lifestyles of everyday people, can highly benefit from partnerships that help them engage with potential customers directly. This includes driving awareness (like we discussed), product discoverability, and encouraging online shopping amongst the target audience. Influencers can also serve as long-term ambassadors for tech, finance, and educational services.

To put this in perspective, let's meet TikTok Content Creator **Everett Noble** (or **@EvcNoble** on all social platforms), most known for his viral comedy sketches. After joining TikTok in 2019 and teaching himself to write, direct, and edit his own videos that tackle real life moments through a comedic lens, Everett has grown his social reach to over 10 million people on TikTok, Instagram, and YouTube combined. Currently holding a top spot amongst gen z creators, he has partnered with brands like Cash App and Converse who find this audience highly attractive to create content around their products and services.

MEDIA CHANNELS:

With millions of people using social media to consume content worldwide, owning a go-to media channel is a very lucrative opportunity. Whether you like to live-tweet while binge-watching your favorite shows, host live streams, or highlight popular culture moments through video clips, memes, and images—there is plenty of room to find your lane on social media. Channel archetypes include Twitter and Instagram communities, YouTube shows, podcasts, and blogs. These avenues generate revenue through sponsored posts, brand mentions, affiliate links, and more.

A great example of this, is the Instagram community known as **@Slam** or 'The Basketball Bible". This platform covers all things basketball; from game highlights, locker room interviews, exclusive pics, and even fashion content on its brother platform, **@LeagueFits**. Anyone passionate about sports culture can own and operate a media property like this. Additionally, you can get paid to partner with people and consumer brands who see value and getting in front of your niche audience.

MUSIC & ENTERTAINMENT
PARTNERSHIPS:

Influencers can also partner with entertainment brands like record labels, tv and film networks, and on-demand streaming services that want to reach audiences through targeted campaigns. Brands will primarily choose to work with voices that are the most relevant and have a noticeable passion for entertainment and popular culture. This presents opportunities to engage with super-fan communities through sponsored posts and real-time activations. Such as advanced screenings, launch parties, live panel discussions, and social challenges. Once again, these tactics help brands win attention and start online conversations.

I'm personally very impressed by **Logitech x Billboard's Song Breaker Chart** (the first-ever creator-centered music chart) driven by influencers who play a role in driving music discovery and turning songs into hits. Creators like **@UsimMango** (4.5M+ followers), **@CityBoyJ** (1.1M+ followers), and **@JuucyJ** (1.5M+ followers) are known for sparking virality through music-based content. This makes them the ideal partners for record labels or independent artists who want a strong push behind a new music release. In my experience, music and entertainment campaigns typically have smaller influencer marketing budgets than consumer goods campaigns.

PODCASTS & LIVE STREAMING:

If people listen when you speak, you might want to consider starting a podcast or live stream channel. According to Business Insider, podcasting is projected to reach almost $1.6 billion by 2024. Not only does podcasting create an opportunity for people with dynamic personalities to host passionate conversations, but the audience is large, growing, and more attractive than ever! This means brands are now more willing to spend money on podcast advertising like sponsored pre-rolls (think radio ads) and dedicated episodes if they can ensure that the selected show aligns with the people who are most likely to buy from them. The same goes for live streaming, which is a popular medium heavily used by gamers.

Someone doing this well is Entrepreneur & Podcaster, **David Shands (@SleepIs4Suckers** on Instagram). Coining the phrase "sleep is for suckers", David leveraged his apparel business success story to launch a top podcast in the entrepreneurship category. The **Social Proof Podcast** focuses on introducing entrepreneurs who have built something and have a story that can help other people bridge the gap between their job and their dreams. Additionally, he has built an online community of almost half a million people who loyally support his merch, events, mastermind groups, and book projects. A multi-hyphenate recipe that has made him a very profitable entrepreneur.

At this point you're probably thinking, "Okay, great, but how much do influencers get paid?" The answer is, well, it depends. There are so many factors like industry, **reach**, **impressions**, and **engagement** data that will go into determining your market value. So, without that information, I don't know how much you specifically can charge for partnerships, if at all.

REACH:

is the total number of unique people who see your content.

IMPRESSIONS:

are the number of times your content is displayed, no matter if it was clicked or not.

ENGAGEMENT:

is the measurement of comments, likes, and shares.

Your engagement rate is like your social credit score. It measures the health of your account, by evaluating the average number of interactions your social media content receives per follower. In fact, it's more important than your reach in most cases. To help you further, I have outlined some general industry benchmarks that you can use as a guide to see where you rank.

Tier	Instagram	TikTok	Youtube
Mega	1M+	2.5M+	1M+
Macro	500K - 1M	750K - 2.5M	100K - 1M
Mid-tier	50K -500K	150K -750K	25K -100K
Micro	10K - 50K	50K - 150K	10K - 25K
Nano	1K - 10K	5K - 50K	1K - 10K

To evaluate your earning potential, take the data that you gathered and head over to **fypm.vip**. It's like 'Glassdoor' but for influencers, by influencers. The website allows you to compare and see what other creators are being paid for similar deals and campaigns. You can gauge price points by using crowd sourced data and advice from your creative peers.

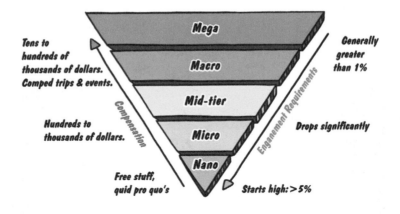

Smaller brands prefer to pay their influencers with free products or samples, rather than paying cash. These types of partnerships are best for influencers who are nano to micro-sized, or want to explore a new relationship with a company they really like. Larger brands do engage non-paid influencers as well, but primarily focus their marketing goals on paid partnerships that move the needle. A brand's purpose for working with influencers is to make a *return on investment* (ROI). Gaining awareness or new followers is great, but the main goal is to see an increase in sales and annual revenue (unless stated otherwise). So, make sure the campaign's goals and KPIs are clear before you say yes.

RETURN ON **INVESTMENT:**

A metric used to understand the profitability of an investment or the ratio between net income and investment.

CHAPTER **SEVEN**

CREATOR ARCHETYPES

The pantheon of influencers has exploded and there is a creator to represent and occupy every imaginable niche in the market. In this chapter we are going to unpack the most common archetypes we see in the creator economy.

THE **STRATEGIST**

THE **CURATOR**

THE **ARTIST**

THE **CAMPAIGNER**

THE **CELEBRITY**

THE **VISIONARY**

THE **ENTERTAINER**

THE **STRATEGIST**

NAME: DGX
PRONOUNS: HE / HIM
PERSONALITY TYPE: ENTJ

DGX is who I identify with most. Born to an Afro-Latino family, he is first-gen innovator who has architected a career as a **marketing strategist**. People like us are more prescriptive and action-oriented than traditional visionaries. We thrive on ideas for adopting strategies that help people and businesses conceptualize their future and think from a place they're desiring to go. You've been learning about my personal journey this entire read. So, let's meet some of the other digital navigators.

THE **CURATOR**

NAME: MAX
PRONOUNS: HE/HIM
PERSONALITY TYPE: INTJ

FAVORITE **CREATOR(S):**

Alton Mason (@AltonMason), Wisdom Kaye (@Wisdm)

Descending from Nigeria, MAX is a fashion shapeshifter who has architected a career as **model** and **style curator**. Serving as his own creative director, stylist, and photographer; MAX has an undeniable taste for menswear that is the cornerstone of his social identity. He is a coveted curator of a cultural niche (i.e. streetwear, luxury fashion, design, food or travel) and his audience looks to him as a source of inspiration for wider fashion trends.

While inside his college dorm room, MAX heard his friends talking about the buzzing social app TikTok, and they later convinced him to compile videos of his experimental outfits. To his amazement, the videos he posted blew up in popularity, taking off on IG Reels first. MAX became so busy creating content, that he decided to take a break from school and focus on his true passion—fashion. Unlike other social media platforms, the 6'1" creator found the aspirational side of TikTok, where the fashion community is all about visual storytelling and unapologetic self-expression.

His fresh and unique take on men's fashion, constantly challenging hyper-masculinity, amassed thousands of followers. Which led to global recognition and partnerships with top fashion brands in the industry.

CREATOR **TIP**:

Use social media as a tool to create content around something that you already do, naturally. Whether your thing is fashion, cooking, or painting the goal should be to document who you are and not who you're pretending to be. Post upwards of 2-3 times per day to maximize your organic reach. Between main feed, stories, tweets, and blog posts it's very possible to publish content at this frequency.

THE **ARTIST**

NAME: FLEX
PRONOUNS: HE/HIM
PERSONALITY TYPE: ISFP

FAVORITE CREATOR(S):

Kristopher Kites (@Kristopher.Kites), Selehe Bembury (@SaleheBembury), Christopher John Rogers (@ChristopherJohnRogers)

Growing up in New York completely immersed in art and fashion, **FLEX** architected a career as a **multifaceted designer**. Spending more time on photoshop than on social media, the artist archetype benefits from a passionately engaged audience who are eager to share their favorite creator's content and purchase their next-level creations.

FLEX was always drawn to things that allowed him to express himself nonverbally. Heavily inspired by human emotion, cartoon characters, and the costumes he saw in comic books, a collection designed by FLEX is built with the intention of turning individuality into a superpower. His main claim to fame is the themed streetwear and jewelry pieces he creates, turning imaginary characters and concepts into wearable art. After studying Industrial Design at Parsons, FLEX applied for the CFDA fashion calendar to get his name out there. Fortunately, he won the CFDA/

Vogue Fashion Fund, an Anna Wintour-led endeavor that acts as a fast lane for putting emerging designers on the map. He used the money to move his dream forward. Kickstarting his career on Instagram, FLEX translated his pieces into visually stunning content to create hype and capture the attention of audiences alike. He used DMs to connect with other creators and eventually got his work in the hands of some of the biggest athletes and entertainers in the world.

CREATOR TIP:

Identify the resources available in your industry (i.e. Accelerator Programs or Fashion Funds) that foster not only creative talent, but also the entrepreneurial spirit needed to succeed in today's landscape. Once you feel confident about your product, one of the best public relations strategies is to get it in the hands of people who fit the profile of your ideal client. Gifting other creators or celebrities in exchange for a social media post is a proven and effective way to drive awareness for your brand. Consider including a personal note and a unique hashtag people can use when sharing your work online.

THE **CAMPAIGNER**

NAME: JAXN

PRONOUNS: HE/HIM

PERSONALITY TYPE: INFP

FAVORITE CREATOR(S):

Jahkil Jackson (@JahkilJackson), Orion Jean (@Orion_Monaco_Jean), Isaiah Russell-Bailey (@IsaiahRussellBailey)

At the young age of 7, **JAXN** got involved with charity work for the first time to feed the homeless in Downtown Chicago. The experience of seeing people without shelter inspired him to architect a career as a young **philanthropist** and **social activist**. Campaigners radiate empathy and are there for the cause first and social clout second.

Driven, confident, and an excellent example for the next generation at just 13-years old, JAXN has received multiple awards for his work. He has become a hometown hero, inspiring other young people to become philanthropists and own their own after-school businesses. With the entire world going through a pandemic, he relied on social media to build community and grow awareness for his causes. The youngster has hosted virtual donation drives and charity parties through live streams on Instagram and YouTube, attracting hundreds of kids from over sev-

eral countries who want to give back. To date, his projects have donated thousands of dollars to homeless initiatives around the world in partnership with his favorite sustainability brands. As the youngest of the crew, JXN takes pride in using his platform to be an agent of change.

CREATOR TIP:

Social media is a great tool for amplifying a cause. While some people enjoy scrolling for entertainment, others like to discover and join movements they believe in. Take some time to brainstorm ideas and strategies that can be acted upon individually or organized together as a group—allowing people to join a larger effort that is taking place locally or nationally. Practicing activism develops lifelong skills and attitudes that teach people about citizenship and that there is something you can do when faced with injustice. The tactics also bring opportunities for people to read, write, research, think critically, and talk with each other.

THE **CELEBRITY**

NAME: XANDER
PRONOUNS: THEY/THEM
PERSONALITY TYPE: ISFP

FAVORITE CREATOR(S):

Lil Nas X (@LilNasX), IDK (@IDK)

Identifying as non-binary and a lyrical genius, **XANDER** architected a career as a **global pop star**, telling their stories through infectious messaging that has redefined popular culture. The Celebrity has a positive cult following and a widely varied reach that touches the masses.

At one point in life, XANDER was a disadvantaged teenager spending nights on the floor of their brother's Atlanta apartment—and like a lot of teens today, they were never really enthusiastic about school. They occasionally skipped class and were often labeled as a rebel whenever they would have opposing views or refused to fall in line with the conventions of polite society. Another example of leadership failing to reach a black student and making zero effort to understand their story. Therefore, XANDER started to channel their world view through writing. Determined to build a better life after high school, XANDER quit all their jobs to focus on writing and creating music full-time. They recorded original music—sometimes out of closets—

and uploaded them to every music streaming platform, generating major buzz on Soundcloud. XANDER pledges to use their music as a soundtrack to their activism—a fight to change the narrative around being black and queer in America. Through creative videos and musical storytelling, they have become the voice of a fearless generation. Showing people that regardless of your circumstance, it is possible to turn your life around. In the future, XANDER wants to continue to launch purpose-driven projects that elevate the perspective of black youth and amplify underrepresented stories.

CREATOR TIP:

Don't ever think that your messages are not relevant or important. There are new online communities being created every day, where people with similar stories and experiences are coming together to craft new narratives. Whether it's through music, books, short films, or some other creative medium—start telling your story and your audience will find you. Building an intimate community has also become more practicable thanks to features like LinkedIn and Facebook groups, and emerging platforms like Patreon and Discord.

THE **VISIONARY**

NAME: XAN & XION
PRONOUNS: HE/HIM
PERSONALITY TYPE: INTP

FAVORITE CREATOR(S):

Marques Brownlee (@MKBHD), Ryan Johnson (@ RyanRanItUp)

Growing up as black boys in the inner city, **XAN** and **XION** resorted to gaming as a safe place for most of their childhood. They are obsessed with gaming and have above average skills in math and science, that helped them architect careers as **video game developers** and **tech entrepreneurs**. Visionaries gain their influence from highly insightful analyses.

Attending school in the state of Georgia that is well known for its high school Esports programs, XAN identified a problem. The public schools (especially black dominated schools) could not afford to have a well-equipped library for Esports or have a hub where students could participate in the popular competitions. With more research performed by the International Game Developers Association, he also discovered that there are nearly 83% of African American boys that play video games on a weekly basis. However, only 2% actually work in the Esports and gaming industry full-time. Based on these statistics, XAN and his brother

XION were inspired to create a leading tech and gaming career pipeline for students in underserved institutions and at HBCUs (Historically Black Colleges and Universities). The initiative connects directly with students that would like to develop skills in coding, designing video games, and more! They love to host Esports competitions on Twitch, and in their free time they also post tech trends and reviews on YouTube.

CREATOR TIP:

Your industry is not saturated; you just need to find a different problem to solve. Instead of only thinking about how you can add new products to the marketplace, think about how you can carve out space for new audiences to participate. Identify who is missing from the conversation.

THE **ENTERTAINER**

NAME: KING X
PRONOUNS: HE/HIM
PERSONALITY TYPE: ESFP

FAVORITE **CREATOR(S):**

King Vader (@KingVader), King Bach (@KingBach)

Around the age of 11 **KING X** discovered his interest in acting and filmmaking after watching his older cousin make videos for fun. This inspired him to architect a career as an **actor** and **digital-first video creator.** Entertainers thrive on camera with comedic routines, sentimental stories, and fun storytelling. They know how to keep their audiences' attention.

Starting his journey on the OG video entertainment app "Vine", KING X was a huge fan of Internet Personality and Actor "King Bach," from whom he assumed the title of "King." As a high school teen, he began amassing Vine followers, and became extremely popular from a 30-second viral video that leaned into the visibility of a top trend. His over-dramatized version of the popular challenge brought comic relief to how young adults feel navigating the real world, setting the internet on fire. The video racked up millions of views, including a feature on one of the biggest comedy networks in the world. But just when KING X felt like he was being noticed, Vine shut down. Quickly pivot-

ing, the creator repurposed his content on other social platforms to keep his followers engaged. Together with a couple of his friends, he started a film production collective that has since grown into a team filled with various talents. They create skits, short films, and perform stand-up comedy. His creativity and flawless productions earned him lucrative partnerships and opportunities to create projects with major studios and networks. Fulfilling his childhood dreams of becoming an actor, writer, and director.

CREATOR TIP:

The best strategy for launching your career as a creator is to participate in the trends that are native to the community. Thanks to hashtags, 'Explore' and 'For You' pages—it is easier to discover top trends and cultural moments that people are creating around. Practice injecting yourself into the current conversation to establish your presence and authenticity on the social platform of choice.

CHAPTER **EIGHT**

PERSONAL BRAND ARCHITECTURE

Apple challenged the world to "Think Different" and Nike encouraged people, regardless of age, gender, or physical fitness level, to "Just Do It". Over the years, these recognizable slogans have morphed into communities, setting the tone for how each company communicates and identifies itself in the marketplace. In just a handful of words, these tag lines have told a story and influenced how people perceive the organizations and the people behind them. Together, they represent the power and potential of branding.

Branding is what companies stand for. It's reflected in how that company acts, how it serves people, the value that the company shares, and how they present those values. A strong brand stands out in the crowd. It gains more bargaining power, increased awareness, and better consumer experiences as a result. But branding isn't just for companies. We all have our own stories to tell and ideas, skills, and expertise to share. In today's increasingly digital world, a personal brand is no longer a nice-to-have; it's a must-have.

Just as a company's brand helps them to differentiate from the competition, a personal brand does the same for individuals. Helping to communicate a unique identity and clear value proposition to potential community members, partners, clients, or employers. Strategically developing a personal brand through social media works brilliantly for creatives. However, it can work for anyone in any industry who chooses to see its advantage. In fact, an overwhelming number of brand representatives and hiring managers report that a person's brand influences their decision to inquire or do business with them. That is why it is important to build a personal brand that highlights your strengths, establishes your reputation, builds trust, and conveys why you're the obvious choice. If cultivated well, your personal brand will send a pre-qualifying signal of whether or not you'll be the right fit for a particular culture or opportunity. But take your time. Some people choose to work at companies until they build up their knowledge, experience, and savings accounts before taking the entrepreneurial leap. The point is, you are in complete control of how the world sees you, how often, and in what context.

Developing a personal brand might sound challenging, but there are gradual steps you can take to build credibility in your industry.

UNLOCK YOUR STRENGTHS:

Taking a regular inventory of your strengths (and weaknesses) will allow you to become more self-aware and shape your brand identity. To start, I recommend taking a Strengths-Finder test using a service like **HIGH5**. A free strengths test that helps people discover what they are naturally good at.

Be introspective and ask yourself:

- What motivates me?
- What is my talent, and in which areas of work do I excel?
- What characteristics come to mind when I ask close friends and family to describe me?
- What type of work or people seem to drain my energy?
- What projects can I spend hours on without feeling tired or overwhelmed?

Once you're more aware of the different facets of your talent and personality, you can decide how to best build a brand around them. You can create an identity you won't have to fake.

FIND **YOUR NICHE**

Creators that are experiencing success in today's market are cutting through the noise by focusing on **niche** spaces.

NICHE:

A specialized segment of the market for a particular kind of product or service.

The biggest mistake I see a lot of people make is that they lack direction. Meaning, they try to reach everyone instead of focusing on a specific audience or market of people they know they can serve. The sooner you define your audience, the easier it will be to craft your story. You'll better understand what type of story you need to tell and where you need to tell it. When thinking about the niche, you can consider industry (i.e. luxury fashion), demographics (i.e. male, 19-25, professional athletes who are interested in fashion), themes/topics (top high-end menswear brands), and more. From there, spend some time brainstorming how you can add value or solve problems for that particular community. What are they talking about? What types of products are they using and buying?

LEARN **FROM THE BEST:**

Compiling research through books, interviews, and internet searches is the best way to learn who the thought leaders are in your field of interest. Find out if they have information available, or where they contribute their thinking. Look for people who are successful and examine what they're doing. Imitate them, remix their strategy, and offer something better.

Your goal is to stand out—but you can't rise to the top without assessing who's already there.

PRACTICE **YOUR PITCH:**

As you begin to package your brand, spend some time crafting your elevator pitch (a 30 to 60-second story about who you are). Whether you're attending an industry event or connecting with someone virtually, having a short pitch prepared makes it easy to describe what you do and where you're going when someone takes an interest in you. The more connections you make (and the more value you can provide in your interactions) the more likely it is that your brand will stick. Considering about 80% of your opportunities will come from your network, getting good at this will help you not only build your brand, but potentially advance your career, too.

GROW YOUR **ONLINE PRESENCE:**

To get the most out of your brand, it is imperative that you build an online presence people can engage with. With so many different social media tools available today, how you approach this will likely look different depending on the medium you choose. Once you know where your targeted audience is most likely to respond, you can focus your efforts on telling your best story there.

PACKAGE **YOURSELF:**

Suppose you are trying to impress existing clientele or attract new customers. In that case, you might choose to tell your story via a personal website or portfolio, where you can better express your wide range of talents and display samples of your work. Website links and portfolios (or pitch decks) are easy to attach to emails and share on the spot. Additionally, I recommend you set up profiles on every social media platform that make sense for the type of content you create and your audience.

The next chapter will give you some platform-specific tips to help you effectively transfer your brand online.

CHAPTER **NINE**

THE NEXT GENERATION OF SOCIAL MEDIA

Next-gen audiences are consistently creating the future and defining trends on social media. The online world is where creators, tastemakers, and niche communities are key to the creation of the new mainstream. Whether you like to talk about music, fashion, creator culture and celebs, beauty, or social justice; social apps regularly unlock new features that allow users to find their own flow and personalize their creator experience. Let's dive into the internet's biggest trends and best practices that will be helpful as you think about your strategy.

TOP **TRENDS**

FASHION & **SHOPPING:**

Traditional shopping is moving away from big online retailer sites. More than half of young people are keeping up with their fashion interests on Instagram and shopping directly through their social media feeds. Now is the time to introduce bold new fashion or start that merch line you've been thinking about.

MUSIC & **DANCE:**

Short-form video is redefining music discovery, and musical experiences are growing in demand on non-traditional music platforms like Instagram and TikTok. With more people expecting to discover new music and artists through social media, the category will evolve into more visual experiences and dance challenges.

CELEBRITIES & **CREATOR CULTURE:**

Social media creators have risen to the level of A-list celebrities. Keeping it short and sweet, this just lets you know that there is room for every voice, regardless of the size of your following.

BEAUTY & GROOMING:

As people become more aware of what they put on their bodies, skincare is a growing trend. There is a lane wide open for boys to experiment with "clean" makeup and grooming products.

WELLNESS:

Young people are connecting (and rethinking) how choices they're making in their lives have powerful effects on their emotional health. As a result, they are leaning into creative and mental wellness activities like at-home workouts, guided meditation, manifestation exercises, painting, writing, and more. There is so much opportunity in the holistic wellness space.

GAMING & DIGITAL ART:

Due to quarantine, games are becoming a new kind of social platform that fuels deep connections and escapism in a unique and fantastical way. Offering new ways to virtually "hang out" and collide with the world of fashion, games are officially the new mall. We can expect to see more innovation around live streams, Esports, VR concerts, digital-only goods, and of course the METAVERSE. Be an early adopter.

SOCIAL JUSTICE:

Rightfully so, advocates are the most active social users. 52% of young people followed social justice accounts on social media in 2021, reinforcing how integral media is for sharing information on activism. Join the movement of people who are donating their own time, attention, and money to social causes.

INSTAGRAM

With roughly 1.3 billion users to date—Instagram has given people the power to build community, shape culture, and express themselves on a global scale. If you dominate when it comes to producing compelling images and videos, you should be using Instagram as one of your primary content hubs.

GET INSPIRED:

If you need ideas about what to create, try exploring other Instagram accounts to see what people like you are sharing as inspiration. Something that works well is following similar accounts or industry leaders that complement the content style you want to adopt. Additionally, you can search relevant hashtags and save the posts you like to reference later.

BE INTENTIONAL WITH VISUAL AND CAPTIONS:

Think of your Instagram profile like an extension of you (because that's what it is), and share posts that allow viewers to discover your work and establish a connection with you. Your content should visually engage, educate, or excite your audience, while your caption encourages the actions you want people to take, like 'Comment' or 'Check out XYZ".

MAKE VIDEOS:

Instagram heavily prioritizes creators that utilize the video features, especially Instagram Reels, which is a new way to create and discover short entertaining videos on the platform. Reels enables creators to record and edit 15-second multi-clip videos with audio, effects, and new creative tools. Reels can be shared with your followers on Feed, or you can make them available to the wider Instagram community through the Explore page.

SOCIAL TIP:

Hashtags are a great way to increase visibility and capture the attention of brands. If you browse your favorite social media platform, you will notice that most brands have a unique hashtag in their bios. This is their way of saying, "to be a part of our community, use this hashtag".

Social media managers regularly search through these hashtags to find relevant accounts to engage with and source user-generated content to re-share. Consider this when building your social strategy.

Also, did you know that you can follow hashtags? Click a hashtag on Instagram and at the top of the feed, it will allow you to 'follow' and see the many posts associated with that specific hashtag.

HASHTAG:

A metadata tag used on microblogging, photo, and video-sharing services as a form of user-generated tagging that enables cross-referencing of content; that is, sharing a topic or theme.

TIKTOK

TikTok is the latest social media phenomenon that sparked a new creator community during the height of the pandemic in 2020. Also amassing over 1 billion users—TikTok is the go-to platform for sharing and discovering short, entertaining videos that feature singing, dancing, comedy, lip-syncing, fun challenges, and more. Suppose you are ready to move away from just being a spectator online and become a content creator. TikTok might be the platform for you!

LEARN THE NATIVE CULTURE:

TikTok favors an entirely different set of creative "best practices" compared to Instagram. This includes vertical video (square or widescreen shots look very out of place) and content that is typically 60 seconds or less. This is also the platform for unpolished or less-produced content. The videos that perform the best on TikTok are usually shot on the phone (although some people choose to use professional cameras and equipment). Lastly, using new or trending music from the app's built-in library will help boost viewership and engagement.

CREATE **EVERYDAY:**

While you can get away with a few posts, creators that are serious about TikTok post new content daily. Yes, this sounds like a lot, but the good news is that this content is a much lower lift than what you're used to producing for older platforms like YouTube or Instagram. Frequency is essential because of the nature of TikTok's algorithm. While some creators are seeing great organic reach, it's much more sensitive than other platforms'. I've learned from some early adopters that they would post upwards of two to three times a day when first starting out. Even with the best content, it's good to establish a consistent posting schedule.

PARTICIPATE **IN TRENDS:**

If you know anything about TikTok, it's that it's known for launching new trends. Whether it's music, skits, dance challenges, or fashion content; joining these trends is a great way to accelerate the success of your channel. The value here is twofold. First, TikTok's algorithm boosts the exposure of videos participating in what's trending, giving you a lift in viewership via their #ForYou page. And second, your personal brand will benefit from the 'cool' factor of the trend. Hashtag challenges on TikTok are highly visible or top-of-funnel campaigns designed to create buzz, awareness, and affinity. Never has social media offered a way to create a cultural moment on this scale.

COLLABORATE:

I often see that TikTok-first creators experience the most success on the platform. These influencers built their audiences on TikTok (formerly Music.ly) and deeply understand how to drive engagement on the platform. TikTok-native creators also generally have a better handle on viral content and growing their following through entertaining collaborations. A good starting point to discover creators to potentially collaborate with is by browsing hashtags that are related to your interests or specific to your location.

SOCIAL **TIP:**

Don't let disorganization and procrastination be the reason you don't commit to getting active on social media. There are many tools and resources available to help you edit, organize, and publish your content. They will also help you save time and money.

Here is a list of some of my favorite creative tools:

Photo Editing	Video Editing	Websites Builders
Snapseed Facetune Adobe Creative Suite (Photoshop)	InShot Adobe Creative Suite (Premiere)	Wix Squarespace Elementor Editor X Shopify
Logos + Graphics	Content Planning	Reposting
Canva Adobe Creative Suite (Illustrator)	Planoly Hootsuite Later	Repost+

TWITCH

Twitch is more than a live streaming service. It's a place where millions of people come together every day to chat, interact and make their own entertainment together. It differentiates itself from other social networks by prioritizing live video and features that allow people to host intimate music and gaming sessions, cooking and talk shows, Esports tournaments, and more. Twitch is also a developer's dreamland creating a playground for tech enthusiasts to create extensions that enable interactive experiences. Explore Twitch, and you might find your thing as a live personality.

UNDERSTAND THE **CREATOR LEVELS:**

As you grow as a streamer, Twitch equips creators with new features, rewards, and ways to monetize their channel. When getting started, you will be identified as a basic **Streamer** with access to lots of great features like chat, the ability for viewers to follow your channel and visible analytics on your Dashboard. At the second level, you become an **Affiliate** where you'll have even more great tools at your disposal, including a subscription button for fans to support you and a custom emote. Many streamers strive to become an affiliate because it's one step closer to becoming a **Twitch Partner**. This level unlocks many additional creator benefits, including more revenue opportunities and prioritized support.

Requirements	Affiliate	Partner*
Time Streamed (last 30 days)	8 Hours	25 Hours
Unique Days Streamed (last 30 days)	7 Days	12 Days
Average Viewers Per Stream	3 Viewers	75+ Viewers
Followers Reached	50+ Followers	

*Meeting the requirements for Partner does not guarantee Partner status. Once you become eligible, you can submit a Partner application form through your dashboard.

PICK A CATEGORY:

If you were to check out the most popular content on Twitch right now, you'd probably find creators playing games, making art, playing music, cooking, developing new software, or taking their viewers with them on real-life adventures! Your goal should be to carve out a tight-knit corner of the internet to call your own. Top creators build their channels around themes that include displaying skill (in a particular game), providing entertainment, or hosting a social space.

CUSTOMIZE YOUR CHANNEL PAGE:

There are plenty of places on Twitch that can be customized to reflect who you are as a streamer. Take a minute to think about what makes you, your content, or your stream unique. You want your channel page to scream personality and allow others to easily recognize you on the platform.

Areas you can customize to fit your brand are:

Profile Photo	Your profile photo is the image that represents you on your channel page and across Twitch in search, directories, and on the home page.
Channel Banner	Displayed at the top, and most notable on your channel page, your Channel Banner is the background to your hosting, Channel Trailer, and recent broadcast videos.
Profile Biography	Located at the top of the About page, your profile bio should give new viewers a brief introduction to your channel.
Profile Accent Color	This color is displayed when users hover over your channel in directory pages. This is your opportunity to stand out and support your branding with colors unique to you.
Video Player Banner	Also known as the "Offline Image"
Channel Trailer	Available to Partners and Affiliates, you can select a video to introduce yourself to non-followers to see when they stop by your channel if you're offline.
Social Media Links	Displayed in the "About" section next to your Profile Biography, you can select up to 5 social links to support your other social media.
Stream Schedule	You can let viewers know your regular stream times, or your specific stream content for that week by filling out your Stream Schedule.

Emotes	Partners and Affiliates can unlock emotes for their community to use across all of Twitch and as Twitch Stickers on iOS. Along with your emotes, you can also select an emote prefix, which is the 3-6 letter code that goes in front of your emote names. Click on the Default Emotes link to check out some emotes you can use now (until you decide to replace them).
Profile Accent Color	Partners and Affiliates can unlock loyalty badges for long-time subscribers that appear next to the user's name only in that channel's chat.
Cheermotes	For 1, 100, 1000, 5000, and 10,000 levels, Partners can upload custom animated Cheermotes for use in their chats when users choose to use Bits.
Cheer Badges	For 1k up to 5M, Partners and Affiliates can reward users who choose to cheer in their chat with various "Bits Badges".
Cheer Emote Rewards	For 1k up to 5M, Partners a Affiliates can reward users who choose to cheer in their chat by allowing them to permanently unlock an emote when they reach that cheer level.
Channel Points	Partners and Affiliates can enable Channel Points, which allows viewers to accumulate and spend points on fun rewards that seamlessly add to their community experience.

Channel Panels	Shown below your video player and in the "About" section of your channel page, Panels can host any number of extensions or information pieces. From talking about who you are and the content you produce or linking to Affiliate or sponsored opportunities, panels are a great way to provide more information to new viewers about who you are.

STREAM ON SCHEDULE:

Twitch's research on user behavior revealed that most of the content watched on the platform is on a consistent, regular basis. It works just like appointment TV. When you get familiar with a favorite TV show being on at the same time every week, you get annoyed if that programmed time changes suddenly without you knowing it. It's best to stream on a consistent schedule, which means finding the times that work for you throughout the week and sticking to them.

GET TO KNOW **YOUR AUDIENCE:**

You establish the ground rules for your individual community, but everyone who visits your channel plays a part in making it feel like home. So, as a creator, it's important to interact with the living and breathing people who tune in to support you. When viewers are greeted by familiar names in the chat, have their questions answered by you or your moderators, and see others enjoying the stream, it helps build bonds and strengthen subscriber retention.

SOCIAL **TIP:**

Make sure your channel name is the same as your Instagram, TikTok, or Instagram handle. This way viewers can easily find you if they discover your channel outside of Twitch. It's also a good idea to link to your channel directly in the bio of your social media profiles. I recommend branding your channels to your name, that way it still works as you evolve. However, if you choose to go with something more creative, just make sure it makes sense for your brand and the nature of your channel.

LINKEDIN

With 800 million members in more than 200 countries and territories worldwide, LinkedIn serves as a great social media tool for managing your professional identity. It is also the home for decision-makers, corporate executives, entrepreneurs, and employers to connect, collaborate, recruit, and share their thought leadership in a particular industry or area of expertise. Did you know that typically when someone does an online search for an individual, their LinkedIn profile shows up in the top five links on the first page of results? Even without realizing it, your name is already showing up in searches within the platform for individuals and companies looking for people with your knowledge and skills. This means that your LinkedIn profile could be the first and last impression that someone could have of your brand.

Despite having a boring recruitment reputation, LinkedIn is very content-friendly today and should be a top priority. I repeat, this is where a lot of high-level decision-makers and CMOs spend their time. So, if you're currently using the platform as a placeholder for your online resume, make sure it's updated. Your brand is at risk if you are not optimizing all the features that can maximize your visibility on the platform. In my opinion, the best way to use LinkedIn is to document your journey as you go. Update your content regularly and keep your network informed about what's new in your industry, any new skills you've acquired, or recent accomplishments. You want to use LinkedIn as your website to enhance your brand.

COMPLETE YOUR PROFILE:

This might sound obvious, but it's not uncommon for users to leave sections of their LinkedIn profile blank. Viewers want to see what experience you have, your educational background, and a snapshot of your accomplishments, so make sure you're showing the full picture. Upload a current photo that represents the person you are today. LinkedIn users with a visible headshot receive 14 times more profile views than those without. Next, update your headline statement. This is a great place to add your job title and a few buzzwords that tell people what you do, how you do it, and for whom.

FOCUS ON KEY **INDUSTRY SKILLS:**

Talent recruiters will often search for keywords that relate to the role they're trying to fill, so it's important to feature industry terms in your profile (whether in your headline, summary, or job description) and explicitly state your skills. For example, if you're pursuing a communications role, zero in on your area of interest and key qualifications, such as public relations, social media, or project management. For content creators, you can highlight your graphic design skills or production capabilities.

QUANTIFY **YOUR ACCOMPLISHMENTS:**

Saying you're "results-oriented" isn't nearly as effective as your actual results. Quantify your accomplishments, when possible; whether it's the number of games you've built, campaigns you've worked on, or strategic partnerships you've secured. LinkedIn also allows you to add supporting media files to your experience. This could be in the form of videos, images, podcast episodes, certifications, case studies, presentations, you name it— you can add anything that provides social proof of the work that you have done in your career.

SOCIAL TIP:

Social networks like LinkedIn can be used for more than just text-only updates. You can also share media such as videos to take your page from static to energetic. This grabs attention and will boost the chances of broadening your reach. According to LinkedIn's research, other members are 20 times more likely to re-share a video on their personal feed than any other type of post.

Here are some thought-starters for your first video:

- **Introduction Video or Virtual Bio:** This allows your audience to match your face to your personality and feel like they are meeting you in person.
- **Spotlight Content:** Document your process and take your audience into your professional world.
- **Social Proof:** Post a physical sample of what you can do and use it to land your next gig.

When you start sharing content on LinkedIn, you can turn your posts into 'featured' posts, which enables specific content to show up on the top of your profile page. If you post something that has valuable information or highlights your best work, feature it so that anyone that comes across your page for the first time can access it.

A PEEK INTO THE METAVERSE

The future of the internet is here, and it's called the metaverse. The next evolution of social connection.

The metaverse is essentially a merging of virtual, augmented, and physical reality. It blurs the line between your interactions online and offline. The conversation has exploded ever since Mark Zuckerberg announced that Facebook would be changing its name to Meta, and investing at least $10 billion on research and developing new products specifically for the metaverse. As more people begin to educate themselves on a future embedded in the metaverse, businesses have already begun to test new ventures.

3D spaces in the metaverse will let you socialize, learn, collaborate, and play in ways that go beyond what we can imagine. It's also a place where users can create, buy, and sell digital-only goods. In the more idealistic visions of the metaverse, it's **interoperable**, allowing you to take virtual items like clothes or cars from one platform to another. In the real world, you can buy a sweatshirt from the mall and then wear it to a concert. Right now, most platforms have virtual identities, avatars, and inventories that are tied to just one platform. The metaverse might allow you to create a persona that you can take everywhere. As easily as you can copy your profile picture from one social network to another.

INTEROPERABLE:

(of computer systems or software) able to exchange and make use of information.

This creates a huge opportunity for visual artists and designers who want to create intellectual property that they can monetize long-term. Some creators like **@Mc-Flyy** (Visual Artist & Graphic Designer) are launching collectible digital art pieces in the form of **NFTs**. Big brands like Nike are also jumping on board, creating new jobs, and investing in digital artists who are already innovating in the space. The metaverse will be a collective development that goes beyond a single company. It will be created by people all over the world and play a huge role in bridging the gap between brands and fans—allowing them to be a part of the action via **social tokens**. Content creators can use the tokens they issue in two self-reinforcing ways: to build and reward their fan community and to compensate themselves for their creative work. Most frequently, fans buy tokens, but some artists give them away to loyal fans. As community members, fans receive benefits such as unique content, access to group chats or exclusive merchandise. Generally, different ownership levels receive different benefits.

Additionally, this innovation will enable a new type of creator who loves to build virtual worlds where people can share experiences with one another. Connecting is evolving and so are we.

NFT:

A non-fungible token (NFT) is a unique and non-interchangeable unit of data stored on a blockchain, a form of digital ledger. NFTs can be associated with reproducible digital files such as photos, videos, and audio.

SOCIAL **TOKENS:**

A type of cryptocurrency that a brand, community, or influencer can use to monetise themselves beyond the typical means.

CHAPTER **TEN**

BRAND PARTNER$HIPS

In this chapter, I will break down strategies for monetizing your personal brand (name, image, and likeness) and social media channel. As well as a step-by-step approach to getting your first (or next) brand partnership.

Today, most social platforms have built-in monetization tools that allow creators to earn money from their content. Creators receive funds based on a variety of factors, including the number of views their videos generate (and the authenticity of those views), the level of engagement on their content, paid subscriptions from their superfans, and more. No two creators are the same so this will look different for everyone.

Here is a closer look at ways to monetize per platform:

- **Instagram In-Stream Video Ads and Reels Bonuses:** When you monetize content on Instagram, you are giving brands the ability to promote themselves within the videos you create. Most creators receive a percentage (55% as of 3/2022) of the ad revenue generated per view that will be paid monthly. Instagram has invested over $1 Billion in incentivized programs for creators to cash in on their talents.

- **TikTok Creator Fund:** Creators who follow community guidelines, are at least 18 years old, and have at least 10,000 followers and 100,000 video views (in the last 30 days) are eligible for the Creator Fund. It is not a grant or ad revenue sharing program.

- **Twitch Partner:** On Twitch, creators can earn money several different ways. They can enable subscriptions (or subs) that allows a viewer to pay per month to support their channel. They can find fun ways to integrate Bits into their streams, where viewers can gift them with small financial rewards. Lastly, they can enable ads or earn referral revenue from affiliate links.

The above tools are evolving by the day, but most creators aim to score brand deals as they typically have higher payouts. So that is what I will discuss in this next section.

First and foremost, it is vital that when you are considering brands to partner with, that you lead with purpose. Boring I know, but that should drive your strategy. Influencers that endorse any and everything can come off as desperate and it may send a signal that you are only in it for monetary gain. That tells the audience that you are not thinking about their best interest, ultimately, affecting the performance of your campaigns. When brands put their heads together and work on a purpose-driven project, something beautiful happens.

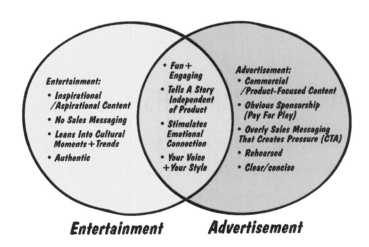

Entertainment:
- Inspirational /Aspirational Content
- No Sales Messaging
- Leans Into Cultural Moments + Trends
- Authentic

- Fun + Engaging
- Tells A Story Independent of Product
- Stimulates Emotional Connection
- Your Voice + Your Style

Advertisement:
- Commercial /Product-Focused Content
- Obvious Sponsorship (Pay For Play)
- Overly Sales Messaging That Creates Pressure (CTA)
- Rehearsed
- Clear/concise

Entertainment   **Advertisement**

It's important to clarify what you wish to gain from a partnership other than money. This starts with analyzing what your business is lacking now (whether it's engagement with a specific community or generating awareness for a cause) and defining how a strategic partnership could help you get there. I repeat don't make it solely about money. A successful collaboration not only gets your brand in front of new audiences, but it also strengthens your brand's reputation in the minds of existing supporters.

Here are some tips on how to build a brand partnership:

MAKE A LIST OF
YOUR IDEAL PARTNERS:

Think beyond content here. These can be brands you want to work with for product endorsements, ambassador programs, or events and social opportunities. You want to have a roster with more than one option or partnership angle. You do not need to approach every brand with a full plan, but you will stand out if you come to the table with thought starters and ideas. Brands are very open to brainstorming with potential partners who are aligned with their long-term goals. So, take some time to find out what's on their road map for the future.

BUILD A TARGET CONTACT LIST:

The key to building relationships with brands is through the people who get paid to find people like you. Like I mentioned in Chapter 5, about 75% of brands dedicated a large budget to influencer marketing in the last year. Using the funds to expand their digital marketing teams or hire influencer marketing agencies to help achieve their goals. These are the people you should be looking for when trying to get connected to a brand.

Starting with the list of ideal partners you created in step one, write down the names and email addresses of all the employees and affiliated agencies whom you think can initiate the relationship. You can start with Instagram; most companies have an email address attached to their profiles that you can use for general inquiries. Secondly, do your research on LinkedIn. You can find employees who work for a specific company by using the filters that allow you to narrow down your search. I recommend filtering by location and using keywords like 'influencer marketing' 'digital partnerships manager' 'social media manager' or 'marketing manager' to find the most relevant person to contact. I would even suggest reaching out to lower-level coordinators too! They are usually easier to get a hold of and are hungrier to make things happen.

DRAFT **A PITCH LETTER:**

Now it's time to reach out to your ideal partners and pitch yourself.

Unless a brand is coming to you directly, you should never expect securing a brand deal to be easy. The best way to pitch a brand is with vision and with proof. Including sample content, audience data, and social insights will best support you with starting the conversation that you want. A large social following is a huge plus, but don't overthink the numbers. Tell your story with conviction and share a creative approach they can't execute without you.

Remember, a partnership with a brand can be much more than just taking a photo holding their product and mentioning it in a caption. For example, if personality is your strength, you can offer to do an Instagram story takeover or host an event. Influencers who are great at building community are just as valuable as those who drive sales. It's up to you to figure out what will get them excited to engage. When your content and messaging are all over the place, it makes it hard for brands to determine whether collaborating with you would make sense for their marketing goals. The products and services you offer should be clearly defined.

NAVIGATION **POINT:**

There isn't a one size fits all approach to cold outreach, but you should be thoughtful about your initial message. Take a moment to write out your answers to these key points and use them to guide your introduction.

This is...
- Who I am (Vision Statement)
- Whom I serve (Target Audience)
- Why I do It (Mission Statement)
- What I offer (Your Priorities)
- How to engage (Opportunities to Participate)

This is a trust-building exercise, so your message needs to be tailored and personalized so that each prospect feels understood and directly spoken to. Subject lines should be personalized and engaging. Emails should be concise and conversational in tone. Show that you understand their mission. Use interactive and engaging content to support your offerings and try not to start with a big ask. Frame your call to action around education, rather than a sales meeting. Once you feel good about it, send it.

Now, just because you reach out to an individual or a brand does not entitle you to a response. You will generally only hear back from about a third of the people you reach out to, so continue to move down your list and cast the widest net possible. This will maximize your chances of connecting with someone who wants to learn more. Make a side note to follow up with the people you didn't hear back from at the top of every quarter.

PREPARE FOR THE MEETING:

If you get a meeting, make sure you research the brand and are knowledgeable of campaigns and initiatives that are already active. It's just like preparing for a job interview. Companies want to feel like you get them and are aligned with their overall vision and purpose. If you are new to this, I recommend not asking for money in the beginning. Not because you're not worth it but because cash-free conversations open the door, while fee requests will require proof of ROI. According to Business Insider, brands are making $4-$6 per $1 spent on influencer marketing. That being said, the value is there but give yourself some time to gain the experience and tangible proof that your brand drives business results.

Each opportunity is different, so once a brand says "Yes, we want to work with you," use your best judgment when determining whether you want to ask for money or not. The benefits of free or in-kind partnerships are that it gives the brand less control over your content and they also cannot hold you too accountable for KPIs or sales goals. A lot of influencers leverage free partnerships to build their credibility and explore new relationships. If you are being paid, brands have some say-so around creative guidelines, sponsorship disclosures, and what benchmarks they want you to hit to deem your partnership successful. Never go into a paid deal without a signed agreement or without setting the terms upfront. This includes a clear outline of the campaign **deliverables**, **KPIs**, **project timelines**, **usage rights,** and **payment terms**.

DELIVERABLE:

A tangible or intangible good or service produced as a result of a project that is intended to be delivered to a customer.

KEY PERFORMANCE INDICATOR:

The critical indicators of progress toward an intended result. KPIs provide a focus for strategic and operational improvement, create an analytical basis for decision making, and help focus attention on what matters most.

PROJECT TIMELINE:

A comprehensive visual overview of a project that paints a roadmap for your project with milestones, tasks, dependencies, and delivery dates.

USAGE RIGHTS:

Rights granted to an individual by an artist or creator to use something for a specific purpose and for a particular time.

PAYMENT **TERMS:**

The conditions surrounding the payment part of a sale, typically they specify how much time the buyer has to make payment on the purchase.

If you don't feel quite ready to approach a brand directly, joining an influencer marketing platform or agency may be a good option for you.

Here are some of the best platforms to start exploring:

Influencer Marketing Platforms		
Activate	Obviously	Socialyte
Tribe	Aspire IQ	Viral Nation
Collectively	Open Influence	Fanbytes
Fohr	HireInfluencer	#paid

CHAPTER **ELEVEN**

SIGNING OFF

Okay, so we've reached the finish line. You now know that creativity has power and can open so many doors for you if you let it. I believe in you, but I am also not here to lead you down a false path. Success takes a shit load of work and talent has very little value without patience and persistence. The people who ultimately break through are those who get this, go for their dreams, and play the game with integrity.

Somewhere out there is a kid in middle school who doesn't know that he can turn his obsession for Japanese manga into a streetwear brand like **@JordanBentley** (Founder of Hypland). A department store salesclerk who has the face and moves to be a fashion muse like **@AltonMason** (4x winner of Model.com's 'Model of the Year'). There may be a medical student who is reading this book and thinking, "I'm committed to my profession, but I want to use what I know to educate my community. I'm going to start a TikTok channel and become the next **@JoelBervell**" (TikTok's Medical Mythbuster).

It's unreal what you will discover about yourself when you move from just being a student of manifestation and start doing the work. Life won't necessarily become easier, (there's nothing easy about becoming a full-time influencer or Entrepreneur) but you can create a life with more flexibility and fun. My final message is don't hesitate to take action because you think social media will go away one day. It's not going anywhere. Think about the fact that practically everyone above the age of 13 in America owns a cell phone. As long as we exist, humans will continue to embrace whatever innovations bring the world closer together and encourage community and connection.

P.S.

After you head over to SupportCreativeBlackBoys.org to grab your merch in support of the community, pass this book on and remember to #SupportCreativeBlack-Boys.

Made in the USA
Monee, IL
21 August 2022

11932219R00075